The Prepoceros Rhinoceros:

Nouns of Assemblage in The Animal Kingdom

by
Graham Hastings
Illustrations by Mark Grundig

HUTTON ELECTRONIC PUBLISHING
SOUTHPORT

Copyright 2014 by Graham Hastings
No part of this book may be reproduced, stored in a retrieval system or transmitted by any means (electronic, mechanical, recording, photocopy or otherwise) without written permission from the author or publisher.

ISBN # 978-0-9888775-9-7

Illustrations by Mark Grundig
Interior Design by Katie Johnson

Published by
Huttonelectronicpublishing.com
4147 Carlyle Place; Southport, N.C. 28461
Manufactured in the United States of America

Table of Contents

Animals

A Crash of Rhinoceroses
The Rhinoceros by Ogden Nash 2

A Flock of Sheep
Little Lamb by William Blake 3

A Mob of Kangaroos
The Duck and the Kangaroo by Edward Lear 4

A Herd of Elephants
The Elephant by Hilaire Belloc 6

A Pack of Wolves
The Law of the Jungle by Rudyard Kipling 7

A Flange of Baboons
The Silly Old Baboon by Spike Milligan 8

A Business of Ferrets
A Trip Across the Sea by Anonymous .. 10

A Leap of Leopards
The Snow Leopard by Jason Gray 12

A Pod of Whales
Whales Weep Not! by D. H. Lawrence 13

A Labor of Moles
A Handy Mole by Christina Rosetti 14

A String of Ponies
The Horse's Prayer by Anonymous 16

A Zeal of Zebras
The Zebra by Roy Campbell 17

A Wilderness of Monkeys
Five Little Monkeys Jumping on a Bed, Early Nursery Rhyme 18

A Drift of Swine
The Lady that Loved a Swine by Anonymous 20

A Clutter of Cats
Pussy Cat, Pussy Cat from 'Mother Goose' 21

A Cete of Badgers
Badger by John Clare 22

A Litter of Puppies
The Power of the Dog by Rudyard Kipling 23

A Rag of Colts
The Runaway by Robert Frost 24

A Sleuth of Bears
'Fuzzy Wuzzy' Traditional 26

A Tribe of Goats
The Goat Paths by James Stephens 27

A Scurry of Squirrels
The Squirrel by Anonymous 28

Birds

A Bevy of Swans
*The Wild Swans at Coole by
William Butler Yeats* 30

An Exaltation of Larks
*The Lark Ascending
by George Meredith* 32

An Ostentation of Peacocks
Peacock Display by David Wagoner ... 33

A Party of Jays
A Party of Jays by Emily Dickenson.... 34

A Murder of Crows
Two Old Crows by Vachel Lindsay...... 36

A Pandemonium of Parrots
*Mother Parrot's Advice to Her Children,
African Anonymous* 368

A Parliament of Owls
Five Little Owls by Anonymous 39

A Dissimulation of Birds
Hope by Emily Dickenson................... 40

A Siege of Herons
*The Herons of Elmwood
by Henry Wadsworth Longfellow* 41

A Conspiracy of Ravens
The Raven by Edgar Allen Poe............ 42

A Clamor of Rooks
The Rooks by Arthur Rimbaud............. 43

A Brace of Pheasants
*The Pheasant and the Lark
by Jonathan Swift*............................... 44

A Skein of Wild Geese
*Something Told the Wild Geese
by Rachel Field*................................... 46

A Covey of Quails
Quail's Nest by John Clare 47

A Murmuration of Starlings
The Starling by Amy Lowell................. 48

A Walk of Snipe
Snipe, from the Japanese 49

A Fall of Woodcock
*Death of King George V
by John Betjeman*................................ 50

Fish

A Hover of Trout
*The Song of the Wandering Aengus
by W. B. Yeats*..................................... 52

A Battery of Barracudas
The Barracuda by John Gardner......... 53

A Pod of Porpoises
*A Porpoise With a Purpose
by John T. Baker* 54

A School of Fish
Our Biggest Fish by Eugene Field...... 55

A Grist of Flies
The Fly by William Blake 57

An Army of Ants
Departmental by Robert Frost............ 58

A Cluster of Spiders
*A Noiseless Patient Spider
by Walt Whitman*................................. 60

A Swarm of Bees
*Extract from The Prophet
by Khalil Gibran*.................................. 61

Reptiles

A Quiver of Cobras
The Cobra by Ogden Nash 63

A Turn of Turtles
The Little Turtle by Vachel Lindsay...... 64

A Rumba of Rattlesnakes
*The Mad Gardener's Song
by Lewis Carroll* 65

A Knot of Toads
Toads by Philip Larkin......................... 66

Appendix

The Goat Paths *by James Stephens*....69

The Law of the Jungle
Rudyard Kipling 72

Whales Weep Not!
by D. H. Lawrence............................... 76

The Power of the Dog
by Rudyard Kipling. 78

The Horse's Prayer *by Anonymous* ..80

The Lark Ascending
by George Meredith............................ 83

The Herons of Elmwood
. by Henry Wadsworth Longfellow..........88

The Raven *by Edgar Allan Poe*............90

The Pheasant and the Lark
by Jonathan Swift 95

The Porpoise *by John T. Baker* 101

Our Biggest Fish *by Eugene Field*...104

The Mad Gardener's Song
by Lewis Carroll................................106

Animals

The Prepoceros Rhinoceros

A *Crash* of Rhinoceroses
The Rhinoceros

The rhino is a homely beast,
For human eyes he's not a feast.
Farewell, farewell, you old rhinoceros,
I'll stare at something less prepoceros.

Ogden Nash

Graham Hastings

A *Flock* of Sheep
Little Lamb

Little Lamb, who made thee?
Dost thou know who made thee?
Gave thee life & bid thee feed
By the stream & o'er the mead;
Gave thee clothing of delight,
Softest clothing, wooly bright;
Gave thee such a tender voice,
Making all the vales rejoice?
Little lamb, who made thee?
Dost thou know who made thee?

Little Lamb, I'll tell thee,
Little Lamb, I'll tell thee:
He is called by thy name,
For he calls himself a Lamb.
He is meek & he is mild;
He became a little child.
I a child & thou a lamb,
We are called by His name.
Little Lamb, God bless thee!
Little Lamb, God bless thee!

William Blake

The Prepoceros Rhinoceros

A *Mob* of Kangaroos
The Duck and the Kangaroo

Said the Duck to the Kangaroo,
'Good Gracious! How you hop!
Over the fields and the water too,
As if you would never stop!
My life is a bore in this nasty pond,
And I long to go out in the world and beyond!
I wish I could hop like you!
Said the duck to the Kangaroo.

'Please give me a ride on your back!'
Said the Duck to the Kangaroo.
'I would sit quite still, and do nothing but "Quack,"'
The whole of the long day through!
Over the land and over the sea; --
Please take me a ride, O do!'
Said the Duck to the Kangaroo.

Said the Kangaroo to the Duck,
'This requires some little reflection;
Perhaps on the whole it might bring me luck,
And there seems but one objection,
Which is, if you'll let me speak so bold,
Your feet are unpleasantly wet and cold,
And would probably give me the roo-
Matiz!' said the Kangaroo.

Graham Hastings

Said the Duck, 'as I sat on the rocks,
I have thought over that completely,
And I bought four pairs of worsted socks
Which fit my web-feet neatly.
And to keep out the cold I've brought a cloak,
And every day a cigar I'll smoke,

All follow my own dear true
Love of a Kangaroo!'

Said the Kangaroo, 'I'm ready!
All in the moonlight pale;
But to balance me well, dear Duck, sit steady!
And quite at the end of my tail!'
So away they went with a hop and a bound,
And they hopped the whole world three times round;
And who so happy, -- O who,
As the Duck and the Kangaroo?

Edward Lear

The Prepoceros Rhinoceros

A *Herd* of Elephants
The Elephant

When people call this beast to mind,
They marvel more and more
At such a little tail behind,
So large a trunk before.

Hilaire Belloc

Graham Hastings

A *Pack* of Wolves
The Law of the Jungle

Now this is the Law of the Jungle – as old and as true as the sky;
And the Wolf that shall keep it may prosper, but the Wolf that shall break it must die.
As the creeper that girdles the tree-trunk, the Law runneth forward and back-
For the strength of the Pack is the Wolf, and the strength of the Wolf is the Pack.

Rudyard Kipling
(fragment, from the Law of the Jungle)
Entire poem in appendix

The Prepoceros Rhinoceros

A *Flange* of Baboons
The Silly Old Baboon

There was a baboon
Who one afternoon
Said I think I will fly to the sun
So with great palms
strapped to his arms
he started his takeoff run.

Mile after mile
He galloped in style
But never once left the ground
You're going too slow said a passing crow
Try reaching the speed of sound

SO

He put on a spurt
My God how it hurt
Both the soles of his feet caught on fire
As he went through a stream
There were great clouds of steam
But he never got any higher

Graham Hastings

On and on through the night
Both his knees caught alight
Clouds of smoke billowed out of his rear!
Quick to his aid
Were the fire brigade
They chased him for over a year

Many moons passed by
Did Baboons ever fly
Did he ever get to the sun
I've just heard today
He's well on his way
He'll be passing through Acton at one.

Spike Milligan

The Prepoceros Rhinoceros

A *Business* of Ferrets
A Trip Across the Sea

If I had to pick but one thing To Take Across the Sea
I think I'd pick a ferret
To go along with me.

A ferret is more precious
Than any other thing
They can make you feel complete
And get your soul to sing.

And when that a ferret and I
Set sail across that sea
We'll fear to squall nor storm
Together strong we'll be.

A ferret is more grounding
Than an anchor or a rope
He can make you safe, secure
And fill your heart with hope.

Graham Hastings

When I've crossed that sprawling sea
And stepped out on new land
I will not be a stranger there
I'll have my ferret in my hand.

A ferret is more rewarding
Than the treasures of the sea
It can give you wealth through love
Your spirit rich and free.

If I had to pick but one thing
To take across the sea
I know I'd pick
A ferret
To go along with me!

Anonymous

The Prepoceros Rhinoceros

A *Leap* of Leopards
The Snow Leopard

He pads on grassy banks behind a fence,
With measured paces slow and tense.

Beyond his cage his thoughts are sharp and white;
He lives a compelled anchorite.

A solid ghost gone blind with all the green,
He waits and waits to be unseen.

Jason Gray

Graham Hastings

A *Pod* of Whales
Whales Weep Not!

All the whales in the wider deeps, hot are they, as they urge
On and on, and dive beneath the icebergs.
The right whales, the sperm-whales, the hammer-heads, the killers

There they blow, there they blow, hot and white breath out of the sea!

D.H Lawrence
(fragment)

The Prepoceros Rhinoceros

A *Labor* of Moles
A Handy Mole

A handy mole who plied no shovel
To excavate his vaulted hovel,
While hard at work met in mid-furrow
An earthworm boring out his burrow.
Our mole had dined and must grow thinner
Before he gulped a second dinner,
And on no other terms cared he
To meet a worm of low degree.

The mole turned on his blindest eye
Passing that base mechanic by;
The worm entrenches in actual blindness
Ignored or kindness or unkindness;
Each wrought his own exclusive tunnel
To reach his own exclusive funnel.

Graham Hastings

A plough its flawless track pursuing
Involved them in one common ruin.
Where now the mine and countermine
They dined-on and the one to dine?
The impartial ploughshare of extinction
Annulled them all without distinction.

Christina Rosetti

The Prepoceros Rhinoceros

A *Strip* of Ponies
The Horse's Prayer

Feed me, water and care for me,
And when the day's work is done
Shelter, a clean, dry bed and
A stall wide enough for me to lie down in comfort.

.
.
.

Remember that I must be ready at any moment
To lose my life in your service

.
.
.

You will not consider me irreverent if I ask this
In the name of HIM who was born in a stable.

Traditional

Graham Hastings

A *Zeal* of Zebras
The Zebra

From the dark woods that breathe of fallen showers,
Harnessed with level rays in golden reins,
The zebras draw the dawn across the plans
Wading knee-deep among the scarlet flowers.
The sunlight, zithering on their flanks with fire,
Flashes between the shadows as they pass
Barred with electric tremors through the grass
Like wind along the gold strings of a lyre.
Into the flushed air snorting rosy plumes
That smoulder round their feet in drifting fumes,
With dove-like voices call the distant fillies,
While round the herds the stallion wheels his flight,
Engine of beauty, volted with delight,
To roll his mare among the trampled lilies.

Roy Campbell

The Prepoceros Rhinoceros

A *Wilderness* of Monkeys
Five Little Monkeys Jumping on a Bed

Five little monkeys jumping on the bed,
One fell off and bumped his head.
Mama called the Doctor and the Doctor said,
"No more monkeys jumping on the bed!"

Four little monkeys jumping on the bed,
One fell off and bumped her head.
Papa called the Doctor and the Doctor said,
"No more monkeys jumping on the bed!"

Graham Hastings

Three little monkeys jumping on the bed,
One fell off and bumped his head.
Mama called the Doctor and the Doctor said,
"No more monkeys jumping on the bed!"

Two little monkeys jumping on the bed,
One fell off and bumped her head.
Papa called the Doctor and the Doctor said,
"No more monkeys jumping on the bed!"

One little monkey jumping on the bed,
He fell off and bumped his head.
Mama called the Doctor and the Doctor said,
"Put those little monkeys straight to bed!"

Traditional
English nursery rhyme

A *Drift* of Swine
The Lady that Loved a Swine

There was a lady loved a swine,
"Honey!" quoth she;
"Pig-hog, wilt thou be mine?"
"Hoogh!" quoth he.

"I'd build thee a silver sty,
"Honey!" quoth she."
"And it in thou shalt lie!"
"Hoogh!" quoth he.

"Pinned with a silver pin,
"Honey!" quoth she;
Thou mayest go out and in,
"Hoogh!" quoth he.

"Wilt thou have me now,
"Honey?" quoth she;
"Speak of my heart will break,"
"Hoogh!" quoth he.

Anonymous

Graham Hastings

A *Clutter* of Cats
Pussy Cat, Pussy Cat

Pussy cat, pussy cat
Where have you been?

I've been to London
To see the Queen.

Pussy cat, pussy cat
What did you there?

I frightened
A little mouse
Under her chair.

Traditional
(from Mother Goose)

The Prepoceros Rhinoceros

A *Cete* of Badgers
Badger

The badger grunting on his woodland track
With shaggy hide and sharp nose scrowed with black
Roots in the bushes and the woods, and makes
A great high burrow in the ferns and brakes.
With nose on ground he runs an awkward race.
The shepherd's dog will run him to his den
Followed and hooted by the dogs and men.

John Clare
(fragment)

Graham Hastings

A *Litter* of Puppies
The Power of the Dog

Buy a pup and money will buy
Love unflinching that cannot lie –
Perfect passion and worship fed
By a kick in the ribs or a pat on the head.
Nevertheless it is hardly fair
To give your love to a dog to tear.

Rudyard Kipling
(fragment)

The Prepoceros Rhinoceros

A *Rag* of Colts
The Runaway

Once when the snow of the year was beginning to fall,
We stopped by a mountain pasture to say 'Whose colt?"
A little Morgan had once forefoot on the wall,
The other curled at his breast. He dipped his head
And snorted at us. And then he had to bolt.
We heard the miniature thunder where he fled,
And we saw him or thought we saw him, dim and gray

Graham Hastings

Like a shadow against the curtain of falling flakes.
'I think the little fellow's afraid of the snow.
He isn't winter-broken. It isn't play
With the little fellow at all. He's running away.
I doubt if even his mother could tell him, "Sakes,
It's only weather." He'd think she didn't know!
Where is his mother? He can't be out alone.'
And now he comes again with a clatter of stone
And mounts the wall again with whited eyes
And all his tail that isn't hair up straight.
He shudders his coat as if to throw off flies.
'Whoever it is that leaves him out so late,
When other creatures have gone to stall and bin,
Ought to be told to come and take him in.'

Robert Frost

The Prepoceros Rhinoceros

A *Sleuth* of Bears
Fuzzy Wuzzy

Fuzzy Wuzzy was a bear
Fuzzy Wuzzy had no hair
Fuzzy Wuzzy wasn't fuzzy
Was he?

Traditional

Graham Hastings

A *Tribe* of Goats
The Goat Paths

The crooked paths go every way
Upon the hill – they wind about
Through he heather in and out
Of the quiet sunniness.
And there the goats, day after day,
Stray to sunny quietness,
Cropping here and cropping there,
As they pause and turn and pass,
Now a bit of heather spray,
Now a mouthful of the grass.

James Stephens

The Prepoceros Rhinoceros

A *Scurry* of Squirrels
The Squirrel

Whisky, frisky,
Hippity hop;
Up he goes
To the tree top!

Whirly, twirly,
Round and round,
Down he scampers
To the ground.

Furly, curly
What a tail!
Tall as a feather
Broad as a sail!

Where's his supper?
In the shell,
Snappity, crackity,
Out it fell.

Anonymous

Graham Hastings

Birds

The Prepoceros Rhinoceros

A *Bevy* of Swans
The Wild Swans at Coole

The trees are in their autumn beauty,
The woodland paths are dry,
Under the October twilight the water
Mirrors a still sky;
Upon the brimming water among the stones
Are nine-and-fifty swans.

The nineteenth autumn has come upon me
Since I first made my count;
I saw, before I had well finished,
All suddenly mount
And scatter wheeling in great broken rings
Upon their clamorous wings.

I have looked upon those brilliant creatures,
And now my heart is sore.
All's changed since, I hearing at twilight,
The first time on this shore,
The bell-beat of their wings above my head,
Trod with a lighter tread.

Graham Hastings

Unwearied still, lover by lover,
They paddle in the cold
Companionable streams or climb the air;
Their hearts have not grown old;
Passion or conquest, wander where they will,
Attend upon them still.

But now they drift on the still water,
Mysterious, beautiful;
Among the rushes will they build,
By what lake's edge or pool
Delight men's eyes when I awake some day
To find they have flown away?

W. B. Yeats

An *Exaltation* of Larks
The Lark Ascending

......
For singing till his heaven fills,
'T is love or earth that he instills,
And ever winging up and up,
Our valley is his golden cup,
And he the wine which overflows
To lift us with him as he goes

George Meredith
(fragment)

Graham Hastings

An *Ostentation* of Peacocks
Peacock Display

He approaches her, trailing his whole fortune,
Perfectly cocksure, and suddenly spreads
The huge fan of his tail for her amazement.

Each turquoise and purple, black-horned, walleyed quill
Comes quivering forward, an amphitheatric shell
For his most fortunate audience: her alone.

He plumes himself. He shakes his brassily gold
Wings and rump in a dance, lifting his claws
Stiff-legged under the great bulge of his breast.

And she strolls calmly away pecking and pausing
Not watching, astonished to discover
All these seeds spread just for her in the dirt.

David Wagoner

The Prepoceros Rhinoceros

A *Party* of Jays
The Blue Jay

No brigadier throughout the year
So civic was the jay.
A neighbor and a warrior too,
With shrill felicity.

Pursuing winds that censure us
A February day,
The brother of the universe
Was never blown away.

The snow and he are intimate;
I've often seen them play
When heaven looked upon us all
With such severity.

Graham Hastings

I felt apology were due
To an insulted sky,
Whose pompous frown was nutriment
To their temerity.

The pillow of this daring head
Is pungent evergreens;
His larder – terse and militant –
Unknown, refreshing things;

His character a tonic,
His future a dispute;
Unfair an immortality
That leaves his neighbor out.

Emily Dickenson

The Prepoceros Rhinoceros

A *Murder* of Crows
Two Old Crows

Two old crows sat on a fence rail.
Two old crows sat on a fence rail,
Thinking of effect and cause,
Of weeks and flowers,
And nature's laws.
One of them muttered, one of them stuttered,
One of them stuttered, one of them muttered.
Each of them thought far more than he uttered.
One crow asked the other a riddle.
One crow asked the other crow a riddle:
The muttering crow
Asked the stuttering crow,
"Why does a bee have a sword to his fiddle?
Why does a bee have a sword to his fiddle?"
"Bee-cause," said the other crow
Bee-cause
BBBBBBBBBBBBBBB-cause."

Graham Hastings

Just then a bee flew close to their rail: --
Buzzzzzzzzzzzz   zzzzzzz zzzzzzz ZZZZZZZ."
And those two black crows
Turned pale,
And away those crows did sail.
Why?
BBBBBBBBBBBBBBB-cause
BBBBBBBBBBBBBBB- cause
Buzzzzzzzzzzzzzz   zzzzzzzzzzzzzzzz ZZZZZZ

Vachel Lindsey

The Prepoceros Rhinoceros

A *Pandemonium* of Parrots
Mother Parrot's Advice to Her Children

Never get up till the sun gets up,
Or the mists will give you a cold.
And a parrot whose lungs have once been touched
Will never live to be old.
Never eat plumbs that are not quite ripe
For perhaps they will give you a pain.
And never dispute what the hornbill says,
or you'll never dispute again.
Never despise the power of speech:
Learn every word as it comes,
For this is the pride of the parrot race,
That it speaks in a thousand tongues.
Never stay up when the sun goes down,
But sleep in your own home bed,
And if you've been good, as a parrot should,
You will dream that your tail is red.

African, Anonymous

Graham Hastings

A *Parliament* of Owls
Five Little Owls

Five little owls in an old elm tree,
Fluffy and puffy as owls could be,
Blinking and winking with big round eyes
At the big round moon that hung in the skies.

As I passed beneath, I could hear one say,
"There'll be mouse for supper, there will, today!"
Then all of them hooted "Tu-whit, Tu-whoo!"
"Yes, mouse for supper," Hoo hoo, Hoo ho!

Anonymous

The Prepoceros Rhinoceros

A *Dissimulation* of Birds
Hope

Hope is a thing with feathers
That perches in the soul,
And sings the tune – without the words,
And never stops at all.

And sweetest in the gale is heard;
And sore must be the storm
That could abash the little bird
That kept so many warm.

I've heard it in the chilllest land,
And on the strangest sea;
Yet never, in extremity,
It asked a crumb of me.

Emily Dickenson

Graham Hastings

A *Siege* of Herons
The Herons of Elmwood

·········
Sing of the air; and the wild delight
Of wings that uplift and wings that uphold you,
The joy of freedom, the rapture of flight
Through the drift of the floating mists infold you.

Of the landscape lying so far below,
With its towns and rivers and desert places;
And the splendor of light above, and the glow
Of the limitless, blue, ethereal spaces.

Ask him if songs of the Troubadours,
Or of Minnesingers in old black-letter,
Sound in his ears more sweet than yours,
And if yours are not sweeter and wilder and better.

Henry Wadsworth Longfellow
(fragment)

The Prepoceros Rhinoceros

A *Conspiracy* of Ravens
The Raven

But the Raven, sitting lonely on the placid bust, spoke only
That one word, as if his soul in that one word he did outpour.
Nothing further then he uttered – not a feather then he fluttered –
Till I scarcely more than muttered "Other friends have flown before –
On the morrow he will leave me as my hopes have flown before."
Then the bird said "Nevermore."

Edgar Allen Poe
(fragment)

Graham Hastings

A *Clamor* of Rooks
The Rooks

Lord, when the meadowland is cold,
and when the downcast hamlets the long Angeluses are silent,
down on Nature barren of flowers let
them sweep from the wide skies, the dear delightful rooks.

Strange army with your stern cries,
the cold winds are assaulting your nests!
You – along yellowed rivers, over the roads with their old Calvarys,
over ditches, over holds – disperse! And rally!

In your thousands, over the fields of France
where the day before yesterday's dead are sleeping, wheel in wintertime, won't you,
so that each traveler may remember!

Be, then, the one who calls men to duty.
O funeral black bird of ours!
But, ye saints of the sky,
at the oak tree top
the masthead lost in the enchanted twilight,
leave alone the warblers of May, for the sake of those whom,
in the depths of the wood,
in the undergrowth from which there is no escaping
defeat without a future has enslaved.

Arthur Rimbaud

The Prepoceros Rhinoceros

A *Brace* of Pheasants
The Pheasant and the Lark

A pheasant lord, above the rest,
With every grace and talent blest
Was sent to sway, with all his skill,
The scepter of a neighbouring hill.
No science was to him unknown,
For all the arts were all his own:
In all the living learned read
Though more delighted with the dead:
For birds, if ancient tales say true,
Had them their Popes and Homers too;
Could read and write in prose and verse,
And speak like ----, and build like Pearce.
He knew their voices and their wings,
Who, smoothest soars, who sweetest sings;
Who tells with ill-fledged pens to climb,
And who attain'd the true sublime.

Graham Hastings

Their merits he could well descry,
He had so exquisite an eye;
And when that fail'd to show them clear,
He had as exquisite an ear;
It chanced as on a day he stray'd
Beneath an academic shade,
He liked, amidst a thousand throats,
The wildness of a thousand throats,
The wildness of a Woodcock's notes.
And search'd and spied, and seized his game,
And took him home and made him tame;
Found him on trial true and able,
So cheer'd and fed him at his table.

Jonathan Swift
(fragment)

The Prepoceros Rhinoceros

A *Skein* of Wild Geese
Something Told the Wild Geese

Something told the wild geese
It was time to go,
Though the fields lay golden
Something whispered 'snow.'

Leaves were green and stirring,
Berried, luster-glossed,
But beneath warm feathers
Something cautioned "frost."

All the sagging orchards
Steamed with amber spice,
But each wild breast stiffened
At remembered ice.

Something told the wild geese
It was time to fly,
Summer sun was on their wings,
Winter in their cry.

Rachel Field

Graham Hastings

A *Covey* of Quails
Quail's Nest

I wandered out one rainy day
And heard a bird with merry joys
Cry 'wet my foot' for half the way;
I stood and wondered at the noise.

When from my foot a bird did flee –
The rain flew bouncing from her breast
I wondered what the bird could be
And almost trampled on her nest.

The nest was full of eggs and round –
I met a shepherd in the vales,
And stood to tell him what I found
He knew and said it was a quail's.

For he himself the nest had found,
Among the wheat and on the green,
When going on his daily round
With eggs as many as fifteen.

Among the stranger birds they feed,
Their summer flight is short and low,
There's very few know where they breed
And scarcely any where they go.

John Clare

The Prepoceros Rhinoceros

A *Murmuration* of Starlings
The Starling

Forever the impenetrable wall
Of self confines my poor rebellious soul,
I never see the towering white clouds roll
Before a sturdy wind, save through the small
Barred window of my jail. I live a thrall
With all my outer life a clipped, square, hole
Rectangular; a fraction of a scroll
Unwound and winding like a worsted ball.
My thoughts are grown uneager and depressed
Through being always mine, my fancy's wings
Are moulted and the feathers blown away.
I weary for desires never guessed,
For alien passions, strange imaginings,
To be some other person for a day.

Amy Lowell

Graham Hastings

A *Walk* of Snipe
Snipes

autumn evening

in a marsh where snipes fly up

The Haiku

* * * * *

Autumn, Evening Twilight
I am from passions quite immune
Yet something cheerless strikes my heart
In Autumn Evening Twilight, where
The snipe up from the marshes start.

*Translation from
Medieval Japanese*

The Prepoceros Rhinoceros

A *Fall* of Woodcock
Death of King George V

Spirit of well-shot woodcock, partridge, snipe
Flutter and bear him up the Norfolk sky;
In that red house in a red mahogany book-case
The stamp collection waits with mounts long dry.

The big blue eyes are shut which saw wrong clothing
And favorite fields and coverts from a horse;
Old men in country houses hear clocks ticking
Over thick carpets with a deadened force;

Old men who never cheated, never doubted,
Communicated monthly, sit and stare
At the new suburb stretched beyond the runway
Where a young man lands hatless from the air.

John Betjeman

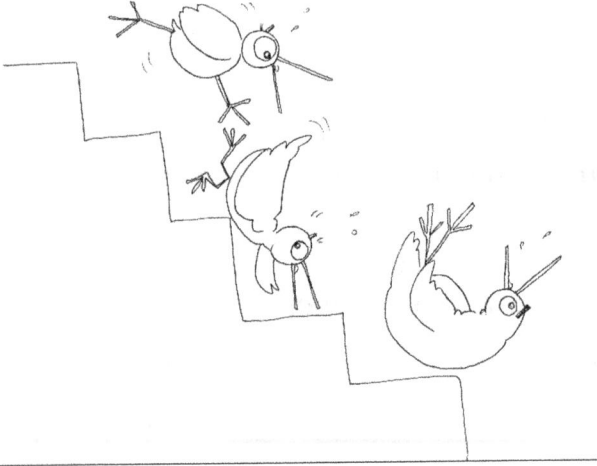

Graham Hastings

Fish

The Prepoceros Rhinoceros

A *Hover* of Trout
The Song of the Wandering Aengus

I went out in the hazel wood
Because a fire was in my head,
And cut and peeled a hazel wand,
And hooked a berry to a thread;
And when white moths were on the wing,
And moth-like stars were flickering out,
I dropped the berry in a stream
And caught a little silver trout.
When I had laid it on the floor
I went to blow the fire aflame,
But something rustled on the floor
And someone called me by name:
It had become a glimmering girl
With apple blossom in her hair
Who called me by my name and ran
And faded through the brightening air.
Though I am old with wandering
Through hollow lands and hilly lands.
I will find out where she has gone,
And kiss her lips and take her hands;
And walk among long dappled grass,
And pluck till time and times are done
The silver apples of the moon
The golden apples of the sun.

W. B. Yeats

Graham Hastings

A *Battery* of Barracudas
The Barracuda

Slowly, slowly, he cruises
And slowly, slowly, he chooses
Which kind of fish he prefers to take this morning;
Then without warning
The Barracuda opens his jaws, teeth flashing,
And with a horrible, horrible grinding and gnashing,
Devours a hundred poor creatures and feels no remorse.
It's no wonder, of course,
That he really ought, perhaps to change his ways.
But (as he says
With an evil grin)
"It's actually not my fault, you see:
I've nothing to do with the tragedy;
I open my mouth for a yawn – ah me ! –
They all
Swim
In."

John Gardner

The Prepoceros Rhinoceros

A *Porpoise* with a Purpose
A Pod of Porpoises

A porpoise with a purpose
Ventured forth one fateful day
To take a trip behind a ship
Away across the bay.

The purpose of that porpoise
Was to find a bite to eat
Among the scraps that just perhaps
Might well provide a treat.
……..

John T. Baker
(fragment)

Graham Hastings

A *School* of Fish
Our Biggest Fish

When in the halcyon days of old, I was a little tyke,
I used to fish in pickerel ponds for minnows and the like;
And oh, the bitter sadness with which my soul was fraught
When, I rambled home at nightfall with the puny string I'd caught!
And oh, the indignation and the valor I'd display
When I claimed that the biggest fish I'd caught had got away!

Eugene Field
(fragment)

The Prepoceros Rhinoceros

Insects

Graham Hastings

A *Grist* of Flies
The Fly

Little Fly
Thy summer's play,
My thoughtless hand
Has brush'd away.

Am not I
A fly like thee?
Or art not thou
A man like me?

For I dance
And drink & sing;
Till some blind hand
Shall brush my wing.

If thought is life
And strength & breath;
And the want
Of thought is death;

Then am I
A happy fly,
If I live,
Or if I die.

William Blake

The Prepoceros Rhinoceros

An *Army* of Ants
Departmental

An ant on the tablecloth
Ran into dormant moth
Of many times his size.
He showed not the least surprise.
His business wasn't with such.
He gave it scarcely a touch,
And was off on his duty run.
Yet if he encountered one
Of the hive's enquiry squad
Whose work is to find out God
And the nature of time and space
He would put him onto the case.
Ants are a curious race;
One crossing with hurried tread
The body of one of their dead
Isn't given a moment's arrest-
Seems not even impressed.
But he no doubt reports to any
With whom he crosses antennae,
And they no doubt report
To the higher-up court.
Then word goes forth in Formic:
"Death's come to Jerry McCormic,
Our selfless forager Jerry.

Graham Hastings

Will the special Janizary
Whose office it is to bury
The dead of the commissary
Go bring him home to his people.
Lay him in state on a sepal.
Wrap him for shroud in a petal.
Embalm him with ichor of nettle.
This is the word of your Queen."
And presently on the scene
Appears a solemn mortician;
And taking formal position,
With feelers calmly atwiddle,
Seizes the dead by the middle,
And heaving him high in the air,
Carries him out of there.
No one stands round to stare.
If is nobody else's affair
It couldn't be called ungentle
But how thoroughly departmental.

Robert Frost

The Prepoceros Rhinoceros

A *Cluster* of Spiders
A Noiseless Patient Spider

A noiseless, patient spider,
I mark'd, where on a little promontory it stood, isolated;
Mark'd how to explore the vacant, vast surrounding
It launch'd forth filament, filament, filament out of itself;
Ever unreeling them – ever tirelessly speeding them.

And you, O my soul, where you sand,
Surrounded, surrounded in measureless oceans of space
Ceaselessly musing, venturing, throwing, - seeking the spheres, to connect them;
Till the bridge you need, be form'd – till the ductile anchor hold;
Till the gossamer thread you fling catch somewhere, O my soul.

Walt Whitman

Graham Hastings

A *Swarm* of Bees
Bees

… And you would ask in your heart,
"How shall we distinguish that which is good in pleasure from that which is not good?"
Go to your fields and your gardens, and you shall learn that is the pleasure of the bee to gather honey of the flower,
But it is also the pleasure of the flower to yield its honey to the bee.
For to the bee a flower is a fountain of life,
And to the flower, a bee is a messenger of love
And to both, bee and flower, the giving and receiving of pleasure is a need and an ecstasy.

People of Orphalese, be in our pleasures like the flowers and the bees.

Khalil Gibran
The Prophet (excerpt)

The Prepoceros Rhinoceros

Reptiles

Graham Hastings

A *Quiver* of Cobras
The Cobra

This creature fills its mouth with venom
And walks upon its duodenum.
He attempts to tease the cobra
Is soon a sadder he, and sobra.

Ogden Nash

The Prepoceros Rhinoceros

A *Turn* of Turtles
The Little Turtle

There was a little turtle.
He lived in a box.
He swam in a puddle.
He climbed on the rocks.

He snapped at a mosquito.
He snapped at a flea.
He snapped at a minnow.
And he snapped at me.

He caught the mosquito.
He caught the flea.
He caught the minnow.
But he didn't catch me.

Rachel Lindsay

Graham Hastings

A *Rumba* of Rattlesnakes
The Mad Gardener's Song

He thought he saw a Rattlesnake
That questioned him in Greek:
He looked again, and found it was
The Middle of Next Week.
'The one thing I regret,' he said,
'Is that it cannot speak!"

Lewis Carroll

The Prepoceros Rhinoceros

A *Knot* of Toads
Toads

Why should I let the toad *work*
Squat on my life?
Can't I use my wit as a pitchfork
And drive the brute off?

Why should I let the toad work
Squat on my life?
Can't I use my wit as a pitchfork
And drive the brute off?

Six days of the week it soils
With its sickening poison –
Just for paying a few bills!
That's out of proportion.

Lots of folk live on their wits:
Lecturers, lispers,
Losers, loblolly-men, louts-
They don't end their lives as paupers.

Lots of fold live up lanes
With fires in a bucket,
Eat windfalls and tinned sardines,
They seem to like it.

Graham Hastings

Their nippers have got bare feet,
Their unspeakable wives
Are skinny as whippets – and yet
No one actually *starves*.

Ah, were I courageous enough
To shout, 'Stuff your pension!'
But I know, all too well, that's the stuff
That dreams are made on:

For something sufficiently toad-like
Squats in me, too;
It hunkers are heavy as hard luck
And cold as snow,

And will never allow me to blarney
My way of getting
The fame and the girl and the money
All at one sitting.

I don't say, one bodies the other
One's spiritual truth;
But I do say it's hard to lose either,
When you have both.

Philip Larkin

The Prepoceros Rhinoceros

Appendix

Graham Hastings

The Goat Paths

The crooked paths go every way
Upon the hill – they wind about
Through the heather in and out
Of the quiet sunniness.
And there the goats, day by day
Stray in sunny quietness,
Cropping her and cropping there,
As they pause and turn and pass,
Now a bit of heather spray,
Now a mouthful of the grass.

In the deeper sunniness,
In the place where nothing stirs,
Quietly in the quietness,
In the quiet of the furze,
For a time they come and lie
Staring on the roving sky.

The Prepoceros Rhinoceros

If you approach they run away,
They leap and stare, away they bound,
With a sudden angry sound,
To the sunny quietude;
Crouching down where nothing stirs
In the silence of the furze,
Crouching down again to brood
In the sunny solitude

If I were as wise as they,
I would stray apart and brood,
I would beat a hidden way
Through the quiet heather spray
To a sunny solitude;

And should you come I'd run away,
I would make an angry sound,
I would stare and turn and bound
To the deeper quietude,
To the place where nothing stirs
In the silence of the furze.

Graham Hastings

In that airy quietness
I would think as long as they;
Through the quiet sunniness
I would stray away to brood
By a hidden, beaten way
In the sunny solitude.

I would think until I found
Something I can never find,
Something lying on the ground,
In the bottom of my mind.

James Stephens

The Prepoceros Rhinoceros

The Law of the Jungle
(from The Jungle Book)

Now this is the Law of the Jungle –
as old and as true as the sky;
And the Wolf that shall keep it may prosper,
but the Wolf that shall break it must die.

As the creeper that girdles the tree-trunk
the Law ruunneth forward and back –
For the strength of the Pack is the Wolf
and the strength of the Wolf is the Pack.

Wash daily from nose-tip to tail-tip;
drink deeply, but never too deep;
And remember the night is for hunting,
and forget not the day is for sleep.

The Jackal may follow the Tiger,
but, Cub, when they whiskers are grown,
Remember the Wolf is a Hunter –
go forth and get food of thine own.

Keep peace with the Lords of the Jungle –
the Tiger, the Panther, the Bear.
And trouble not Hathi the Silent,
and mock not the Boar in his lair.

Graham Hastings

When Pack meets with Pack in the Jungle,
and neither will go from the trail,
Lie down till the leaders have spoken –
it may be fair words will prevail.

When he fight with a Wolf of the Pack,
ye must fight him alone and afar,
Lest others take part in the quarrel,
and the Pack be diminished by war.

The Lair of the Wolf is his refuge,
and where he has made him his home,
Not even the Head Wolf may enter,
not even the Council may come.

The Lair of the Wolf is his refuge,
but where he has digged it too plain,
The Council shall send him a message,
and so he shall change it again.

The Prepoceros Rhinoceros

If ye kill before midnight, be silent,
And wake not the woods with your bay,
Less ye frighten the deer from the crop
And your brothers go empty away.

Ye may kill for yourselves, and your mates,
and your cubs as they need, and ye can;
But kill not for pleasure of killing,
and seven times never kill Man!

If ye plunder his Kill from a weaker,
devour not all in thy pride;
Pack-Right is the right of the meanest;
so leave him the head and the hide.

The Kill of the Pack is the meat of the Pack.
Ye must eat where it lies;
And no one may carry away of that meat to his lair
or he dies.

To Kill of the Wolf is the meat of the Wolf.
He may do what he will;
But, till he has given permission,
the Pack may not eat of that Kill.

Graham Hastings

Cub-Right is the right of the Yearling.
From all of his Pack he may claim
Full-gorge when the killer has eaten;
and none may refuse him the same.

Lair-Right is the right of the Mother.
From all of her year she may claim
One haunch of each kill for her little,
and none may deny her the same.

Cave-Right is the right of the Father –
To hunt by himself for his own:
He is freed of all calls to the Pack
he is judged by the Council alone.

Because of his age and his cunning,
because of his gripe and his paw,
In all that the Law leaveth open,
the word of your Head Wolf is Law.

Now these are the Laws of the Jungle,
And many and mighty are they;
But the head and the hoof of the Laws
And the haunch and the bump is – Obey!

Rudyard Kipling

The Prepoceros Rhinoceros

Whales Weep Not!

They say the sea is cold, but the sea contains
the hottest blood of all, and the wildest, the most urgent.

All the whales in the wider deeps, hot are they, as they urge
on and on, the dive beneath the icebergs.
The right whales, the sperm-whales, the hammer-heads, the killers
there they blow, there they blow, hot , wild white breath out of the sea!

And they rock and they rock, through the sensual ageless ages
On the depths of the seven seas,
and through the salt the reel with drunk delight
and in the tropics tremble they with love
and roll with massive, strong desire, like gods.
Then the great bull lies up against his bride
in the blue deep bed of the sea,
as mountain pressing on mountain, in the zest of life:
and out of the inward roaring of the inner red ocean of whale-blood

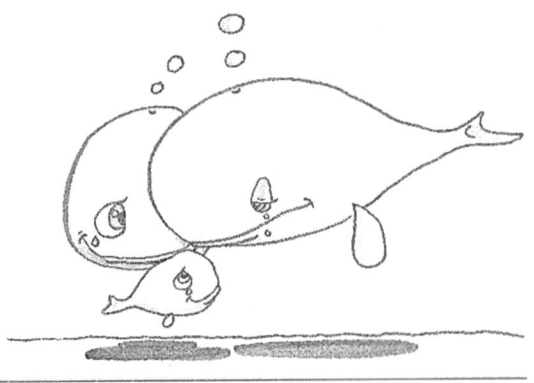

Graham Hastings

the long tip reaches strong intense, like the maelstrom-tip and comes to rest
in the clasp and the soft, wild clutch of a sea-whale's fathomless body.

And over the bridge of the whale's strong phallus, linking the wonder of whales
the burning archangels under the sea keep passing, back and forth,
keep passing, archangels of bliss
from him to her, from her to him, great Cherubim
that wait on whales in mid-ocean, suspended in the waves of the sea
great heaven of whales in waters, old hierarchies.

And enormous mother whales lie dreaming suckling their whale-tender young
and dreaming with strange whale eyes wide open in the waters of the beginning
and the end.

And bull-whales gather their women and whale-calves in a ring
when danger threatens, on the surface of the ceaseless flood
and range themselves like great fierce Seraphim facing the threat
encircling their huddled monsters of love.
and this happens in the sea, in the salt
where God is also love, but without words:
and Aphrodite is the wife of whales
most happy, happy she!

And Venus among the fishes skips and is a she-dolphin
she is the gay, delighted porpoise sporting with love and the sea
she is the female tunny-fish, round and happy among the males
and dense with happy blood, dark rainbow bliss in the sea.

D. H. Lawrence

The Prepoceros Rhinoceros

The Power of the Dog

There is sorrow enough in the natural way
From men and women to fill our day.
But when we are certain of sorrow in store
Why to we always arrange for more?
Brothers and sisters I bid you beware
Of giving your heart to a dog to tear.

Buy a pup and your money will buy
Love unflinching that cannot lie –
Perfect passion and worship bred
By a kick in the ribs or a pat on the head.
Nevertheless it is hardly fair
To give your heart to a dog to tear.

Graham Hastings

When the fourteen years which Nature permits
Are closing in asthma, or tumor or fits,
And the Vet's unspoken prescription runs
To lethal chambers or loaded guns.
Then you will find – it's your own affair
But…you've given your heart to a dog to tear.

When the body that lived at your single will
When the whimper of welcome is stilled (how still!)
When the spirit that answered your every mood
is gone wherever it goes – for good,
You will discover how much you care.
And you will give your heart to a dog to tear!

We've enough sorrow in the natural way
When it comes to burying Christian clay.
Our lives are not given, but only lent,
At compound interest of cent per cent.
Though it is not always the case, I believe,
That the longer we've kept 'em the more we do grieve:
For when debts are payable, right or wrong,
A short term loan is as bad as a long.
So why in Heaven (before we are there!)
Should we give our hearts to a dog to tear?

Rudyard Kipling

The Prepoceros Rhinoceros

The Horse's Prayer

To thee, my master, I offer my prayer.

Feed me, water me and care for me.
And, when the day's work is done, provide me with
shelter, a clean, dry bed and
a stall wide enough to lie down in comfort.

Always be kind to me.
Your voice often means as much to me as the reins.
Pet me sometimes, that I may serve you the more
gladly and learn to love you.

Do not jerk the reins and do not whip me when going uphill.
Never strike, beat, or kick me
when I do not understand what you want,
but give me a chance to understand you.
Watch me, and if I fail to do your bidding,
see if something is not wrong with my harness or feet.

Do not check me so that I cannot have free use of my head.
If you insist I wear blinders,
so that I cannot see behind me as it was intended I should,
I pray you be careful that the blinders stand well out of my eyes.

Do not overload me,
or hitch me where water will drip on me.

Graham Hastings

Keep me well shod.

Examine my teeth when I do not eat; I may have an ulcerated tooth,
and that, you know, is very painful.

Do not tie my head in an unnatural position,
or take away my best defense against flies and
mosquitoes by cutting off my tail.

I cannot tell you when I am thirsty,
so give me clean, cool water often.

Save me by all means in your power
From that fatal disease - ganders.

I cannot tell you in words when I am sick,
so watch me, that by signs you may know my condition.

Give me all possible shelter from the hot sun,
and put a blanket me, not when I am working,

The Prepoceros Rhinoceros

But when I am standing in the cold.
never put a frosty bit in my mouth;
first warm it by holding it a moment in your hands.

I try to carry you and your burden without a murmur,
and wait patiently for you long hours of the day or night.

Without the power to choose my shoes or path,
I sometimes fall on hard pavement which I have often prayed
might not be of wood but of
such nature as to give me a safe and sure footing.

Remember that I must be ready at any moment
To lose my life in your service.

And finally, OH MY MASTER,
when my useful strength is gone,
do not turn me out to starve or freeze,
or sell me to some cruel owner
to be slowly tortured and starved to death;

But do thou, My master, take my life in the kindest ways
and your God will reward you here and in the hereafter.

You will not consider it irreverent if I ask this
in the name of HIM who was born in a stable.

Anonymous

Graham Hastings

The Lark Ascending

He rises and begins to round,
He drops the silver chain of sound
Of many links without a break,
In chirrup, whistle, slur and shake,
All intervolv'd and spreading wide,
Like water-dimples down a tide
Where ripple ripple overcurls
And eddy into eddy whirls;
A press of hurried notes that run
So fleet they scarce are more than one,
Yet changingly the trills repeat
And linger ringing while they fleet.
Sweet to the quick o' ear, and dear
To her beyond the handmaid ear,
Who sits beside our inner springs,
Too often dry for this he brings,
Which seems the very jet of earth
At sight of sun, her music's mirth,
As up he wings the spiral stair
A song of light and pierces air
With fountain ardor, fountain play,
To reach the shining tops of day,
And drink in everything discern'd

The Prepoceros Rhinoceros

An ecstasy to music turn'd,
Imnmpell'd by what his happy bill
Disperses; drinking, showering still,
Unthinking save that he may give
His voice the outlet, there to live
Renew'd in endless notes of glee,
So thirsty of his voice is he,
For all to hear and all to know
That he is joy, awake, aglow,
The tumult of the heart to hear
Through pureness filter'd crystal-clear,
And know the pleasure sprinkled bright
By simple singing of delight,
Shrill, irreflective, unrestrain'd,
Rapt, ringing on the jet sustain'd
Without a break, without a fall,
Silvery sweet, sheer lyrical,
Perennial, quavering up the chord
Like myriad dews of sunny sward
That trembling into fullness shine,
And sparkle dropping argentine;
Such wooing as the ear receives
From zephyr caught in choric leaves
Of aspens when their chattering net
Is flush'd to white with shivers wet;
And such the water-spirit's chime

Graham Hastings

On mountain heights in morning's prime,
Too freshly sweet to seem excess,
Too animate to need a stress;
But wider over many heads
The starry voice ascending spreads,
Awakening, as it waxes thin,
The best in us to him akin;
And every face to watch him rais'd,
Puts on the light of children prais'd,
So rich our human pleasure ripes
When sweetness on sincereness pipes,
Though nought be promis'd from the seas,
But only a soft-rufflling breeze
Sweep glittering on a still content
Serenity in ravishment.

For singing till his heaven fills,
'T is love of earth that he instills,
And ever winging up and up
Our valley is his golden cup,
And he the wine which overflows
To lift us with him as he goes;
The woods and brooks, the sheep and kine
He is, the hills, the human line,
The meadows green, the fallows brown,
The dreams of labor in the town;

The Prepoceros Rhinoceros

He sings the sap, the quicken'd veins;
The wedding song of sun and rains
He is, the dance of children, thanks
Of sowers, shout of primrose-banks,
And eye of violets while they breathe;
All these the circling song will wreathe,
And you shall hear the herb and tree,
The better heart of men shall see,
Shall feel celestially, as long
As you crave nothing but the song,
Was never voice or ours could say
Our inmost in the sweetest way,
Like yonder voice aloft, and link
All hearers in the song they drink;
Our wisdom speaks from failing blood,
Our passion is too full in flood,
We want the key of his wild note
Of truthful in a tuneful throat,
The song seraphically free
Of taint of personality,
So pure that it salutes the suns
The voice of one for millions,
In whom the millions rejoice
For giving their one spirit voice.

Graham Hastings

Yet men we have, whom we revere,
Now names, and men still housing here,
Whose lives, by many a battle-ding
Defaced, and grinding wheels on flint,
Yield substance, though they sing not, sweet
For songs our highest heaven to greet:
Whom heavenly singing gives us new,
Enspheres them brilliant in our blue,
From firmest base to farthest leap,
Because their love of Earth is deep,
And they are warriors in accord
With life to serve and pass reward,
So touching purest and so heard
In the brain's reflex of yon bird;
Wherefore their soul in me or mine,
Through self-forgetfulness divine,
In them, that song aloft maintains,
To fill the sky and thrill the plains
With showerings drawn from human stores,
As he to silence nearer soars,
Extends the world at wings and dome,
More spacious making more our home,
Till lost on his aerial rings
In light, and then the fancy sings.

George Meredith

The Prepoceros Rhinoceros

The Herons of Elmwood

Warm and still in the summer night,
As here by the river's brink I wander;
White overhead are the stars, and white
The glimmering lamps on the hillside yonder.

Silent are all the sounds of day;
Nothing I hear but the chirp of crickets,
And the cry of the herons winging their way
O'er the poet's house in the Elmwood thickets.

Call to him herons, as slowly you pass
To your roosts the haunts of the exiled thrushes,
Sing him the song of the green morass;
And the tides that water the reeds and rushes.

Sing him the mystical Song of the Hern,
And the secret that baffles our utmost seeking;
For only a sound of lament we discern,
And cannot interpret the words you are speaking.

Sing of the air and the wild delight
Of wings that uplift and winds that uphold you,
The joy of freedom, the rapture of flight
Through the drift of the floating mists that infold you.

Graham Hastings

Of the landscape lying so far below,
With its towns and rivers and desert places;
And the splendor of light above and the glow
Of the limitless, blue, ethereal spaces.

Ask him if songs of the Troubadours,
Or of Minnesingers in old black-letter,
Sound in his ears more sweet than yours,
And of yours are not sweeter and wilder and better.

Sing to him, say to him, here at his gate
Where the boughs of the stately elms are meeting,
Some one hath lingered to meditate,
And end him unseen this friendly greeting;

That many another hath done the same,
Though not by a sound was the silence broken;
The surest pledge of a deathless name
Is the silent homage of thoughts unspoken.

Henry Wadsworth Longfellow

The Prepoceros Rhinoceros

The Raven

Once upon a midnight dreary, while I pondered weak and weary,
Over many a quaint and curious volume of forgotten lore,
While I nodded, nearly napping, suddenly there cam a tapping,
As of some one gently rapping, rapping at my chamber door.
'Tis some visitor,' I muttered, 'tapping at my chamber door –
Only this and nothing more.'

As, distinctly I remember it was in the bleak December,
And each separate dying ember wrought its ghost upon the floor.
Eagerly I wished the morrow; - vainly I had sought to borrow
From my books surcease of sorrow – sorry for the lost Lenore –
For the rare and radiant maiden whom the angels name Lenore –
Nameless here forevermore.

And the silken sad uncertain rustling of each purple curtain
Thrilled me – filled me with fantastic terrors never felt before;
So that now, to still the beating of my heart, I stood repeating
'Tis some visitor entreating entrance at my chamber door –
Some late visitor entreating entrance at my chamber door; -
This it is, and nothing more.'

Graham Hastings

Presently my soul grew stronger, hesitating then no longer,
'Sir,' I said, 'or Madam, truly your forgiveness I implore;
But the fact is I was napping, and so gently you came rapping,
And so faintly you came tapping, tapping at my chamber door,
That I scarce was sure I heard you,' – here I opened wide the door –
Darkness there, and nothing more.

Deep into the darkness peering, long I stood there wondering, fearing,
Doubting, dreaming dreams no mortal ever dared to dream before;
But the silence was unbroken, and the darkness gave no token,
And the only word there spoken was the whispered word, 'Lenore!'
This I whispered, and an echo murmured back the word, 'Lenore!'

Back into the chamber turning, all my soul within me burning,
Soon again I heard a tapping somewhat louder than before.
'Surely,' said I, 'surely that is something at my window lattice;
Let me see, then, what there is, and this mystery explore; -
Let my heart be still a moment and this mystery explore
'Tis the wind and nothing more!'

Open here I flung the shutter, when, with many a flirt and flutter,
In there stepped a stately raven of the saintly days of yore.
Not the least obeisance made he, not a minute stopped or stayed he;
But, with mien of lord or lady, perched above my chamber door
Perched upon a bust of Pallas just above my chamber door –
Perched, and sat, and nothing more.

The Prepoceros Rhinoceros

Then this ebony bird beguiling my sad fancy into smiling,
By the grave and stern decorum of the countenance it wore,
'Though thy crest be shorn and shaven, thou,' I said, 'art sure no craven.
Ghastly grim and ancient raven wandering from the nightly shore –
Tell me what thy lordly name is on the Night's Plutonian shore!'
Quoth the raven, 'Nevermore.'

Much I marveled this ungainly fowl to hear discourse so plainly,
Though its answer little meaning – little relevancy bore;
For we cannot help agreeing that no living human being
Ever yet was blessed with seeing bird above his chamber door –
Bird or beast above the sculptured bust above his chamber door,
With such a name as 'Nevermore.'

But the raven, sitting lonely on the placid bust, spoke only,
That one word as if his soul in that one word he did outpour.
Nothing further then he uttered – not a feather then he fluttered –
Till I scarcely more than muttered 'Other friends have flown before –
On the morrow he will leave me, as my hopes have flown before.'
Then the bird said, 'Nevermore.'

Startled at the stillness broken by reply so aptly spoken,
'Doubtless,' said I, 'what it utters is its only stock and store,
Caught from some unhappy master whom unmerciful disaster
Followed fast and followed faster till his songs one burden bore –
Till the dirges of his hope that melancholy burden bore
Of 'Never-nevermore.'

Graham Hastings

But the raven still beguiling all my sad soul into smiling,
Straight I wheeled a cushioned seat in front of bird and bust and door,
Then, upon the velvet sinking, I betook myself to linking
Fancy unto fancy, thinking what this ominous bird of yore –
What this grim, ungainly, gaunt and ominous bird of yore
Meant in croaking 'Nevermore.'

Then I sat engaged in guessing, but no syllable expressing
To the fowl whose fiery eyes now burned into my bosom's core;
This and more I sat divining, with my head at ease reclining
On the cushions' velvet lining that the lamp light gloated o'er,
But whose velvet violet liming with the lamp-light gloating o'er,
She shall press, ah, nevermore!

Then, methought, the air grew denser, perfumed from an unseen censer
Swung by Seraphim whose foot-falls tinkled on the tufted floor.
'Wretch!' I cried, 'thy God hath lent thee – by these angels he has sent thee
Respite – respite and nepenthe from thy memories of Lenore!
Quaff, oh quaff this kind nepenthe, and forget this lost Lenore!'
Quoth the raven 'Nevermore.'

'Prophet!' said I, 'thing of evil! – prophet still, if bird or devil! –
Whether tempter sent, or whether tempest tossed thee here ashore,
Desolate yet all undaunted, on this desert land enchanted –
On this home by horror haunted – tell me truly, I implore! –
Is there – *is* there balm in Gilead? – tell me, tell me, I implore!'
Quoth the raven, 'Nevermore.'

The Prepoceros Rhinoceros

'Prophet!' said I, 'thing of evil! – prophet still, if bird or devil!
By that Heaven that ends above us – by that God we both adore –
Tell this soul with sorrow laden if, within the distant Aidenn,
It shall clasp a sainted maiden whom the angels named Lenore –
Quoth the raven 'Nevermore.'

'Be that word our sign of parting, bird or fiend!' I shrieked upstarting –
'Get thee back into the tempest and the Night's Plutonian shore!
Leave no black plume as a token of that lie thy soul has spoken!
Leave my loneliness unbroken! Quit the bust above my door!'
Quoth the raven 'Nevermore.'

And the raven, never flitting, still is sitting, still is sitting
On the pallid bust of Pallas just above my chamber door;
And his eyes have all the seeming of a demon's that is dreaming,
And the lamp-light o'er him streaming throws his shadow on the floor.
And my soul from out that shadow that lies floating on the floor
Shall be lifted – nevermore'

Edgar Allan Poe

Graham Hastings

The Pheasant and the Lark

In ancient times, as bards indite,
(If clerks have conn'd the records right.)
A peacock reign'd whose glorious sway
His subjects with delight obey:
His tail was beauteous to behold,
Replete with goodly eyes and gold;
Fair emblem of that monarch's guise.
And princely ruled he many regions
And statesmen wise, and gallant legions.

A pheasant lord, above the rest,
With every grace and talent blest,
Was sent to sway with all his skill,
The scepter of a neighboring hill.
No science was to him unknown,
For all the arts were all his own:
In all the living learned read,
Though more delighted with the dead:
For birds, if ancient tales say true,
Had their own Popes and Homers, too;
Could read and write in prose and verse.
And speak like ___, and build like Pearce.
He knew their voices, and their wings
Who smoothest soars, who sweetest sings;

The Prepoceros Rhinoceros

Who toils with ill-fledged pens to climb,
And who attain'd the true sublime.
Their merits he could well descry,He had so exquisite an eye:
And when that fail'd to show them clear,
He had as exquisite an ear;
It chanced as on a day he stray'd
Beneath an academic shade,
He liked, admist a thousand throats,
The wildness of a Woodlark's notes.
And search'd and spied, and seized his game,
And took him home and made him tame;
Found him on trial true and able,
So cheer'd and fed him at his table.

Here some shred critic finds I'm caught,
And cries out "Better fed than taught" --- Then
Jests on game and tame and reads.
And jests and so my tale proceeds.

Long had he studied in the wood,
Conversing with the wise and good:
His soul with harmony inspired,
With love of truth and virtue fired:
His bethren's good and Maker's praise
Were all the study of his lays;
Were all his study in retreat,
And now employ'd him with the great.
His friendship was the sure resort

Graham Hastings

Of all the wretched at the court;
But chiefly merit in distress
His greatest blessing was to bless. ---

This fix'd him in his patron's breast,
But fired with all envy all the rest:
I mean that noisy, craving crew,
Who round the court incessant flew,
And prey'd like rooks, by pairs and dozens,
To fill the maws of sons and cousins:
"Unmoved their heart, and chill'd their blood
To every thought of common good,
Confining every hope and care,
To their own low, contracted sphere."
But found it hard to tell you why,
Till how own worth and wit supplied
Sufficient matter to deride:
" 'Tis envy's safest, surest rule,
To hide her rage in ridicule:
The vulgar eye she best beguiles,
When all her snakes are decked with smiles:
Sardonic smiles, by rancour raised!
Tormented most when seeming pleased."
Their spite had more than half expired,
Had he not wrote what all admired;
What morsels had their malice wanted,
But that he build, and plann'd and planted!
How had his sense and learning grieved them,

The Prepoceros Rhinoceros

But that his charity relieved them!

"At highest worth dull malice reaches,
As slugs pollute the fairest peaches:
Envy defames, as harpies vile
Devour the food they first defile."

Now ask the fruit of all his favour---
'He was not hitherto a saver." ---
When then could make their rage run mad?
"Why, what he hoped, not what he had."

"What tyrant e're invented ropes,
Or racks, or rods, to punish hopes?
Th' inheritance of hope and fame
Is seldom Earthly Wisdom's aim;
Of, if it were, is not so small,
But there is room enough for all."

If he but chance to breathe a song,
(He seldom sang, and never long,)
The noisy, rude, malignant crowd,
Where it was high, pronounced it loud:
Plain Trust was Pride, and, what was sillier,
Easy and Friendly was Familiar.

Or, if he tuned his lofty lays
With solemn air to Virtue's praise,
Alike abusive and erroneous,

Graham Hastings

They call'd it hoarse and inharmonious.
Yet so it was to soul like theirs,
Tuneless as Abel to the bears!

A Rook with harsh malignant caw
Began, was followed by a Caw;
(Though some, who would be thought to know,
Are positive it was a crow.)
Jack Daw was seconded by Tit,
Tom Tit could write and so he writ;
A tribe of tuneless praters follow,
The Jay, the Magpie, and the Swallow;
And twenty more their throats to loose,
Down to the witless, waddling Goose.

Some peck's at him, some flew, some flutter'd,
Some hiss'd, some scream'd and others mutter'd:
The Crow, on carrion wont to feast,
The Carrion crow, condem'd his taste:
The Rook, in earnest, too, not joking,
Swore all his singing was but croaking.
Some thought they meant to show their wit,
Might think so still – "but that they writ"—
Could it be spite or envy? – "no—
Who did so ill could have no foe." –
So wise Simplicity esteem'd;
Quite otherwise True Widsom deem'd;
This question rightly understood,

The Prepoceros Rhinoceros

"What more provokes than doing good?
A soul ennobled and refined
Reproaches every baser mind:
As strains exalted and melodious
Make every meaner music odious." –
At length the Nightingale was heard,
For voice and wisdom long revered,
Esteem'd of all the wise and good,
The Guardian Angel of the wood:
He long in discontent retired,
Yet, not obscured, but more admired:
His brethern's servile and souls disdaining,
He lived indignant and complaining:
They now afresh provoke his choler,
(It seems the Lark had been his scholar
A favourite scholar always near him,
And oft had waked whole nights to hear him.)
Enraged he canvasses the matter,
Exposes all their senseless chatter,
Shows him and them in such a light,
As more inflames, yet quells their spite.
They hear his voice and frightened fly
For rage had raised it very high:
Shames by the wisdom of his notes,
They hide their heads, and hush their throats.

Jonathan Swift

Graham Hastings

The Porpoise

A porpoise with a purpose
Ventured forth one fateful day
To take a trip behind a ship
Away across the bay.

The purpose of the porpoise
Was to find a bite to eat
Among the scraps that just perhaps
Might well provide a treat.

The Captain spied the porpoise
But was not at all concerned;
His years at sea were guarantee
Of lessons he had learned.

The Captain was uncertain
What the porpoise planned to do
But nonetheless he made a guess
And notified the crew.

"Now hear your Captain speaking!"
He informed them with a shout,
'Right dead ahead you will discern
A creature with a snout.

The Prepoceros Rhinoceros

That creature is a porpoise
And its purpose I don't know,
But I respect its intellect –
We'll take it nice and slow."

"Don't be so cautious, Captain,"
Loud a bold young fellow cried,
"We'll simply shoot the bloomin' brute!"
The Captain quick replied:

"You NEVER shoot a porpoise
Till its purpose you perceive;
To improvise would be unwise
And frightfully naïve.

The creature might be wounded
And incited to attack;
We must refrain and ascertain
If it would like a snack.

We'll just placate the porpoise
Till its purpose is revealed;
Now go, good chaps, fetch galley scraps;
THEY'll be our battlefield."

Graham Hastings

The crew obeyed the Captain
And dumped out into the sea
The food they found they had not downed,
A tasty potpourri.

"Well done, brave lads, look hearty!"
The Captain gave a cheer;
"We'll soon find out – just watch its snout –
If it will disappear."

The puzzled porpoise pondered
What the fuss was all about
But just adored the smorgasbord
The sailors had tossed out.

Its purpose thus accomplished
Quick the porpoise then withdrew
And it its ears long rang the cheers
Of that triumphant crew.

The Captain proudly postured
And proposed a pithy rhyme:
"A proper bait propitiates
A porpoise every time."

John T. Baker

The Prepoceros Rhinoceros

Our Biggest Fish

When in the halcyon days of old, I was a little tyke,
I used to fish in pickerel ponds for minnows and the like;
And oh, the bitter sadness with which my soul was fraught
When I rambled home at nightfall with the puny string I'd caught!
And, oh, the indignation and the valor I'd display
When I claimed that all the biggest fish I'd caught had got away!

Sometimes it was the rusty hooks, sometimes the fragile lines,
And many times the treacherous reeds would foil my just designs;
But whether hooks or lines or reeds were actually to blame,
I kept right on at losing all the monsters just the same—
I never lost a little fish – yes, I am free to say
It always was the biggest fish I caught that got away.

And so it was, when later on, I felt ambition pass
From callow minnow joys to nobler greed for pike and bass;
I found it quite convenient, when the beauties wouldn't bite
And I returned all bootless from the watery chase at night
To feign a cheery aspect and recount in accents gay
How the biggest fish that I had caught had somehow got away.

Graham Hastings

And really fish look bigger then they are before they're caught
When the pole is bent into a bow and the slender line is taut,
When a fellow feels his heart rise up like a doughnut in his throat,
And he lunges in a frenzy up and down the leaky boat!
Or, you who've been a-fishing will indorse me when I say
That it always is the biggest fish you caught that got away!

'T'is even so in other things – yes in our greedy eyes
The biggest boon is some elusive, never captured-prize;
We angle for the honors and the sweets of human life –
Like fishermen we brave the seas that roll in endless strife;

And then at last, when all is done and we are spent and gray,
We own the biggest fish we've caught are those that got away.

I would not have it otherwise; 't is better there should be
Much bigger fish than I have caught a-swimming in the sea;
For now some worthier one that I may angle for that game –
May by his arts entice, entrap and comprehend the same;
Which having done, perchance he'll bless the man who's proud to say
That the biggest fish he ever caught were those that got away.

Eugene Field

The Prepoceros Rhinoceros

The Mad Gardener's Song

He thought he saw an Elephant,
That practiced on a fife:
He looked again, and found it was
A letter from his wife.
'At length I realize,' he said
'The bitterness of Life!'

He thought he saw a Buffalo
Upon the chimney-piece:
He looked again, and found it was
His Sister's Husband's Niece.
'Unless you leave my house,' he said,
'I'll send for the police!'

He thought he saw a Rattlesnake
That questioned him in Greek:
He looked again, and found it was
The Middle of Next Week.
'The one thing I regret,' he said,
'Is that it cannot speak!'

Graham Hastings

He thought he saw a Banker's Clerk
Descending from the bus:
He looked again and found it was
A Hippopotamus.
'If this should stay to dine,' he said,
'There won't be much for us!'

He thought he saw a Kangaroo
That worked a coffee-mill:
He looked again, and found it was
A Vegetable-Pill.
'Were I to swallow this,' he said,
'I should be very ill!'

He thought he saw a Coach-and-Four
That stood beside his bed:
He looked again, and found it was
A Bear without a Head.
'Poor thing,' he said, 'poor silly thing!
It's waiting to be fed!'

The Prepoceros Rhinoceros

He thought he saw an Albatross
That fluttered round the lamp:
He looked again, and found it was
A Penny-Postage Stamp.
'You'd best get home, he said:
'The nights are very damp!'

He thought he saw a Garden-Door
That opened with a key:
He looked again and found it was
A Double Rule of Three:
'And all its mystery,' he said
'Is clear as day to me!'

He thought he saw an Argument
That proved he was the Pope:
He looked again, and found it was
A Bar of Mottled Soap.
'A fact so dread,' he faintly said,
'Extinguishes all hope!'

Lewis Carroll

www.ingramcontent.com/pod-product-compliance
Lightning Source LLC
Chambersburg PA
CBHW080010050426
12446CB00036B/3303